# Five Ugly Monsters

## by Tedd Arnold

SCHOLASTIC INC.
Cartwheel BOOKS®

New York  Toronto  London  Auckland  Sydney

*To Sean, Justin, Tera, Aaron, Kim, Mike T., Emilee, Laura, Crystal, Nicky,*
*Evan, Erin, Taylor, Joe, Mike J., Benjamin, Krystle, Lindsey, Diana,*
*Daniel, John, Terry, and Mrs. Callas, third grade, 1994*

*— T.A.*

Copyright © 1995 by Tedd Arnold.
All rights reserved. Published by Scholastic Inc.
CARTWHEEL BOOKS and the CARTWHEEL BOOKS logo are registered trademarks of Scholastic Inc.

No part of this publication may be reproduced in whole or in part, or stored in a retrieval system,
or transmitted in any form or by any means, electronic, mechanical, photocopying, recording, or otherwise,
without written permission or the publisher. For information regarding permission,
write to Scholastic Inc., 555 Broadway, New York, NY 10012.

*Library of Congress Cataloging-in-Publication Data*

Five ugly monsters / by Tedd Arnold.
p.   cm.   (Cartwheel Books story corner)
Summary: Contrary to the doctor's orders, from one to five monsters insist on jumping on a child's bed.
ISBN 0-590-22226-0
[1. Monsters—Fiction.   2. Counting.   3. Stories in rhyme.]
I. Title.   II. Series: Story corner.
PZ8.3.A647Fi   1995
[E]—dc20   94-36991   CIP   AC

12   11   10   9   8   7   6   5   4   3   2   1          5   6   7   8   9/9   10/10

Printed in Singapore

First Scholastic printing, September 1995

**F**ive ugly monsters

jumping on the bed.

One fell off and
bumped its head.

Called for the doctor and the doctor said,

"No more monsters jumping on the bed!"

Four ugly monsters

jumping on the bed.
One fell off and
bumped its head.

Called for the doctor and the doctor said,

"No more monsters jumping on the bed!"

# Three ugly monsters

jumping on the bed.
One fell off and
bumped its head.

Called for the doctor and the doctor said,

"No more monsters jumping on the bed!"

Two ugly monsters

jumping on the bed.
One fell off and
bumped its head.

Called for the doctor and the doctor said,

"No more monsters jumping on the bed!"

One ugly monster

jumping on the bed.
It fell off and
bumped its head.

Called for the doctor and . . .

"No more monsters

The end